Water, Water Everywhere

For Jed, Luke, and Mali—J.B.
For Jay, Jeff and Peaches—H.P.

Produced by Daniel Weiss Associates, Inc.
33 West 17 Street, New York, NY 10011
Copyright © 1990 Daniel Weiss Associates, Inc.,
and Al Jarnow.

Illustration copyright © 1990 Heidi Petach

Published by Silver Press, a division of
Silver Burdett Press, Inc., Simon & Schuster, Inc.
Prentice Hall Bldg., Englewood Cliffs, NJ 07632
For information address: Silver Press.

Printed in the United States of America
10 9 8 7 6 5 4 3

Library of Congress Cataloging-in-Publication Data

Barkan, Joanne.
Water, water everywhere / written by Joanne Barkan; illustrated
by Heidi Petach.
p.   cm.—(First facts)
Summary: Explains the origins and uses of water.
1. Water—Juvenile literature.   [1.Water.]   I. Petach, Heidi,
ill.   II. Title.   III. Series: First facts
(Englewood Cliffs, N.J.)
GB662.B37 1989   89-39193
553.7—dc20   CIP
*   AC*
ISBN 0-671-68657-7   ISBN 0-671-68653-4 (lib. bdg.)

First Facts™

Water, Water Everywhere

Written by Joanne Barkan
Illustrated by Heidi Petach

Silver Press

There's water, water everywhere.
Watch it splash against the window
when it rains.

Let it tickle your toes at the beach.

See it sparkle in the pretty fountain.

And when you're thirsty,
turn on the faucet and have a drink!

Why do you feel thirsty sometimes?
Your body is telling you it needs water.
People, animals, and plants need
water to live.

Have you ever seen a plant that
hasn't had enough water?
It looks wrinkled and limp.
Hurry and give that plant a drink!

You probably live on land—
in a city, a town, or in the country.
Almost all people live on land.

But most of the world is covered with water.
And most of the water is in the oceans.
Lakes, rivers, and ponds are filled
with water, too.

Not all water is the same.
Ocean water is very salty.
It's not good for drinking.

Water in lakes and rivers is not salty.
It's called fresh water.
The water you drink everyday is fresh water.

Water is a liquid when it flows.
It takes the shape of whatever
you pour it into.

In a glass, it has the shape of a glass.
If you spill it on the floor—oops!—
it has the shape of a spill!

Here's another riddle.
When is water *neither* a liquid *nor* solid ice?

If you don't know, just try this.
Ask a grown-up to boil some water
on the stove.
As the water boils, you'll see it turn
into water vapor.

Look at the raindrops falling
on a wet day.

Yesterday the drops may have been
in the ocean!
How is this possible?

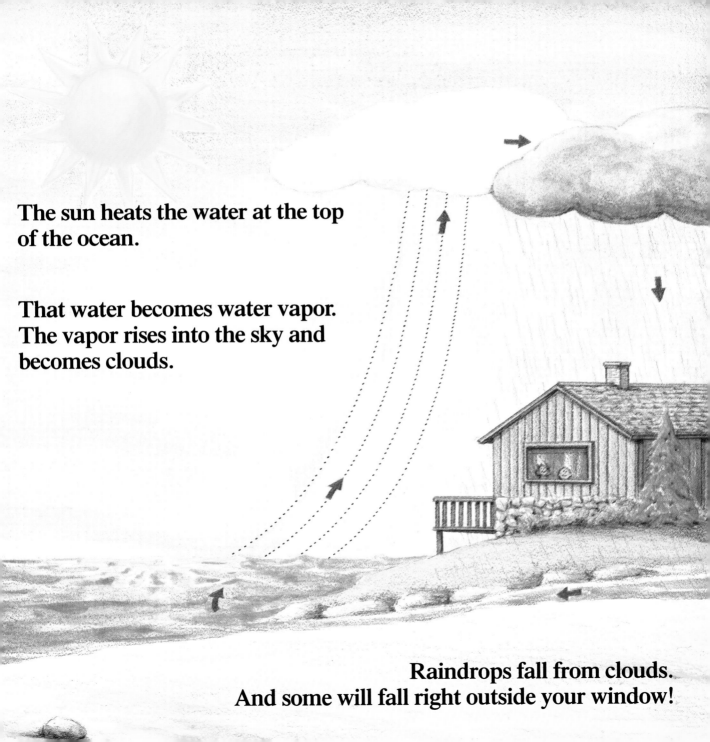

The sun heats the water at the top of the ocean.

That water becomes water vapor. The vapor rises into the sky and becomes clouds.

Raindrops fall from clouds.
And some will fall right outside your window!

At home your family uses water again and again everyday.

Cities and towns get water
from lakes, rivers, and reservoirs.
A reservoir is a lake
that people have made themselves.

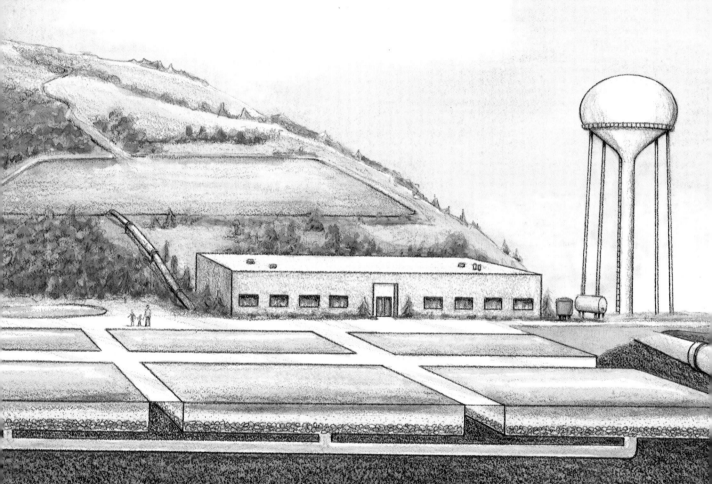

Water is cleaned of all dirt before
it is pumped into a city or town.

Then it runs through big pipes
underneath the streets.
Smaller pipes carry it
into your home.

Water is used in many ways.

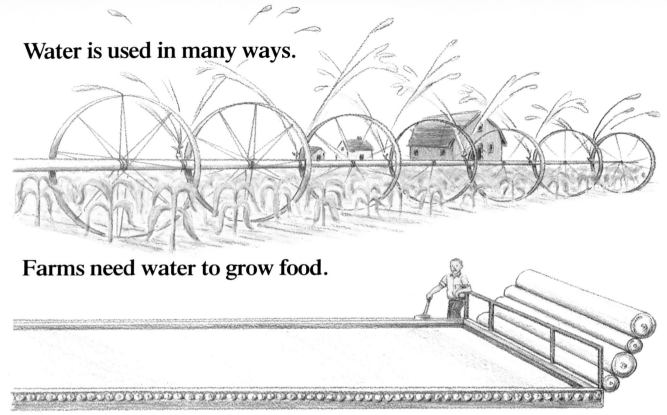

Farms need water to grow food.

Most factories use water to make things.
Water was used to make the paper for this book!

Water is important for traveling.
Boats carry people and things across lakes,
rivers, and oceans.

Water is also used for having fun.

Water must be kept clean if you want to use it.

When garbage is put in lakes, rivers, and oceans, it dirties the water. This is called water pollution.

Everyone must work together
to keep the water clean,
and to try not to waste it.

Some places in the world
get very little rain.
These places are called deserts.
People who live in the desert
must find a way to get water.

Sometimes they pipe it in
from far away.
Sometimes they dig deep holes
until they find water underground.

You can dig your own water hole at the beach.
Try digging a canyon or tunnel, too.

Watch the waves fill everything up.
The water shapes the sand,
and the waves carry some of it away.

Water shapes many wonderful
things in the world.
Rivers carve deep canyons
through mountains and plateaus.

Waves carry sand to the shores
and make beaches.

You can hike along canyons,
and swim along beaches.
You can go fishing in rivers,
and watch the colors of the sun set in a lake.
Aren't you glad there's
water, water everywhere!